FASCINATING

FOR

YEAR OLD KIDS

A Message From the Publisher

Hello! My name is Hayden and I am the owner of Hayden Fox Publishing, the publishing house that brought you this title.

My hope is that you and your young comedian love this book and enjoy every single page. If you do, please think about **giving us your honest feedback via a review on Amazon**. It may only take a moment, but it really does mean the world for small businesses like mine.

Even if you happen to not like this title, please let us know the reason in your review so that we may improve this title for the future and serve you better.

The mission of Hayden Fox is to create premium content for children that will help them increase their confidence and grow their imaginations while having tons of fun along the way.

Without you, however, this would not be possible, so we sincerely thank you for your purchase and for supporting our company mission.

Sincerely,
Hayden Fox

FASCINATING FACTS

MANATEES are believed to account for at least some of the early-explorer's mermaid sightings. They can reach 13-feet long and weigh as much as 3,000 pounds.

Try all you want, but it is impossible to lick your own **ELBOW**

There are over 80,000 narwhals throughout the Arctic waters.

Only about 11% of the world write
LEFT HANDED

The letter **"E"** is the most used
letter in the alphabet.

Contrary to popular belief,
hippopotamus milk is NOT PINK

MONOPOLY is the most played board game in the world.

Buttermilk doesn't actually have any BUTTER in it!

Women blink TWICE as much as men do.

A polar bear's hair appears white due to the way it reflects light, but it is actually COLORLESS . The skin beneath the transparent fur is black, which helps absorb warmth from the sun to keep the bear warm.

MOSQUiTOES can be annoying insects but did you know that it's only the female mosquito that actually bites humans.

Horses and cows sleep standing UP

FOR 8 YEAR OLDS

The **LION** has the loudest roar of all the big cats. It can be heard as far as 5km (3 miles) away.

DIAMONDS are the strongest natural material in the world.

A **BEEFALO** is a domestic animal that is a cross between a domestic cow and a male bison.

The elephant uses its **TRUNK** to know the size, shape, and temperature of objects. It is used to suck in water or pick up food and put it into its mouth.

The Killer Whale or **ORCA** is actually a type of a dolphin.

DOGS have been loyal and useful companions to humans through the ages, providing physical and emotional security as loving pets.

FOR 8 YEAR OLDS

CATS use their whiskers to check whether a space is too small for them to fit through or not.

A **SHARK'S** skeleton is made up of cartilage that is tough and has flexible tissues. There is not a single bone in their bodies.

LIONS have a lifespan of about 10-14 years in the wild.

Just like a human fingerprint, no two giraffes have the same spots on their SKiN

DOLPHiNS are carnivorous animals that feed on fish and other marine animals.

Dolphins use whistling, clicking and other sounds to COMMUNiCATE with each other.

The **CHEETAH** is the fastest animal to roam the earth, with top speeds of 113 km per hour.

Originally **TENNIS** was played with your bare hands, rather than with a racket.

A piece of paper can only be folded **7 TIMES**

Gorillas sleep for about **14** hours per day.

Michael Phelps has won more Olympic gold medals than **MEXICO**

MELBOURNE, in Australia, was the official host city for the 1956 Summer Olympic Games, but it was unable to host the equestrian events due to the country's tough quarantine laws.

SKI BALLET used to be a competitive sport.

The first recorded DIVING championship in the UK took place in 1889. It was called the Championships of Scotland and involved three different types of dives: one from the side of the swimming pool, one from a height of six feet and a surface dive.

The silhouette on the NBA logo is Hall of Fame Laker Jerry West.

Despite being allergic to **CHOCOLATE** Junior had a bar named after him.

The Apollo 14 astronauts participated in what Mitchell later jokingly described as "the first **LUNAR OLYMPICS**"

At one point in August 1971, the Pittsburgh Pirates became the first professional team to field nine players who were either **BLACK** or LATINO

In July of 1934, Babe Ruth paid a fan $20 for the return of the BASEBALL he hit for his 700th career home run.

TUG OF WAR was an Olympic event between 1900 and 1920.

MICHAEL JORDAN was once one of the best high school pitchers in North Carolina.

 Hens lay approximately **228** eggs per year.

It takes **35,000** cows to supply the NFL with enough leather for a year's supply of footballs.

 **GOLF BALLS** can reach speeds of 211 miles an hour.

 **PiTTSBURGH** is the only American city with three sports teams that wear the same colors.

The state sport of Maryland is **JOUSTiNG**

 Babe Ruth wore a CABBAGE leaf under his cap to keep him cool and changed it every two innings.

There are more than **350** dimples on a golf ball. Finally we can stop counting.

In 1910, an incomplete forward pass earned teams a **15-YARD** penalty.

At horse race tracks, the favorite wins about 30 (or less) percent of the time. Clearly the horses start soaking in their own reverence.

A **HEATWAVE** can make train tracks bend!

SOCCER (football) is the most popular sport in the world.

Wildfires sometimes create tornadoes made of fire called **FIRE WHIRLS**

Cats and dogs have been known to sense when a **TORNADO** is approaching.

You can tell the temperature by counting a cricket's CHIRPS

Cow's milk is the most common ALLERGY in the world.

 Some tornadoes can be faster than **FORMULA ONE** racing cars.

The fastest speed a raindrop can hit you is **20 MPH**

 **BLIZZARDS** can make snowflakes feel like pellets hitting your face.

Cirrus clouds are made of ICE crystals.

More than 10 million tons of SALT are used on U.S. roads each winter.

Thunderstorms occur most often in hot and humid environments. These tropical storms can come on quickly and cause major DAMAGE, especially if there is hail combined with strong winds and lightning.

Much like the fire whirl tornadoes can make in hot weather, tornadoes can appear over water too and these are called 'WATERSPOUTS'

TORNADOES (or twisters) are rotating columns of air that start in a storm cloud and reach down to Earth. Winds of a tornado can reach speeds of up to 300 mph!

In the United States there is a place known as **TORNADO ALLEY**, this area between West Texas and North Dakota can have over 200 tornadoes every year!

The deadliest blizzard in recorded history happened in IRAN in 1972 and lasted for almost a week. The snowfall reached 26 feet in some areas and completely enveloped 200 villages in snow.

Large volumes of snow absorb SOUND waves! This explains the eerie silence that can be noticed if you step outside after a heavy snowfall.

Lightning is hotter than the SUN

A **BLIZZARD** is an extreme snow storm, characterized by winds reaching over 35 mph, and less than a quarter of a mile visibility for three hours or more.

There are about **8.6 MILLION** strikes of lightning every day.

WORMS wriggle up to the surface of the earth before a flood.

 The Empire State Building gets struck by lightning about 50 times each year.

Lightning can result in
FOREST FIRES

 The flag of USA has 13 stripes which represent the 13 original states.

Rivers have **FROZEN** due to extremely cold weather.

There is no **SOUND** in space!

The Great Red Spot of Jupiter is a storm that has been raging for over **200** years!

There are more STARS in space than there are grains of sand on a beach!

Venus is named after the Roman god of LOVE

A year on Mercury takes 88 Earth days.

BULLS run faster uphill than downhill.

Mars has **TWO** moons, Phobos and Deimos.

A year on Venus takes 225 Earth days.

Saturn is made mostly of
HYDROGEN

FOUR spacecraft have
visited Saturn.

Neptune is named after the Roman
god of **SEA**

FOR 8 YEAR OLDS

 **SATURN** can be seen with the naked eye.

Pluto is one third **ICE**

 A light year is unit of measurement to measure distance. It is equivalent to the distance that light travels in **1 YEAR**

FOR 8 YEAR OLDS

Nobody truly knows knows how many STARS are in space.

Neutron stars can spin 200 times per second.

The footprints on the Moon will be there for 100 MILLION years.

The Moon has **NO** atmosphere.

In 4.5 billion years the Milky Way and Andromeda galaxies will **COLLIDE**

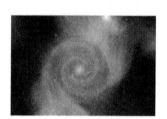

Mercury is still **SHRINKING**

FOR 8 YEAR OLDS

There are mountains on PLUTO

There could be LIFE in the solar system, somewhere. While no definitive evidence of life beyond Earth has been found yet, some scientists believe that it is possible that there could be life on other planets or moons in our solar system or beyond.

URANUS is tilted on its side

The largest known asteroid is **CERES**, which is about 590 miles (940 kilometers) in diameter.

It is a misconception that your average body temperature **DECLINES** as you age.

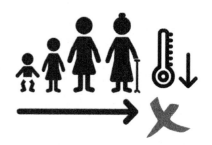

Dogs are only able to sweat through their FEET and TONGUES

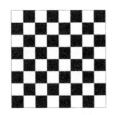 Checkers is older than **CHESS**

CRUSTY eyes in the morning? That will just be your body building up a little collection of tears, mucus, and dead skin cells for you to blearily wipe away!

 Although the bathroom seems like the germy hot spot of the house, the average kitchen sink actually contains **200,000** times more germs!

'Algal bloom', also known as RED tide, is when the algae concentration in water is so high it changes the color. The effects of the red tide can be fatal as it depletes the water of oxygen while it decomposes – deadly and gross!

TV controls are literally swarming with germs, not only are they one of the dirtiest items in the home but one US study discovered that REMOTE controls are the leading carrier of bacteria in hospital rooms!

The size of the Great Barrier Reef is so massive that it can be seen all the way from the MOON

In just seven hours, an elephant can produce a pile of poop that weighs the same as one fully grown **PERSON**

If a cockroach's head comes off its body, the body can still survive for another week without its **HEAD**

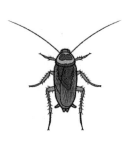

Einstein was a big fan of getting sleep – he slept for 10 hours a day on average, plus he used to take naps during the daytime!

PiLLOWS collect a lot of dust mites and dead skin over the years.

Old cosmetics contain unsafe levels of **BACTERiA**

RACECAR has the same spelling backwards as it does forwards.

The coldest place on the planet is **ANTARCTICA**

Dolphins sleep with one eye **OPEN**

In Italian, the name **PINOCCHIO** means pine eyes.

Tomatoes and avocadoes are considered **FRUITS**, not vegetables.

The inventor of the **PRINGLES** can is now buried in one.

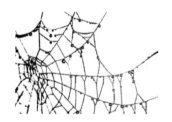

Spider webs were used as **BANDAGES** in ancient times.

Cotton candy was invented by
a **DENTIST**

Disney World is larger than
over **10** countries in the
world.

A cloud can weigh more than
a **MILLION** pounds.

The Queen owns all the **SWANS** in England.

Starfish do not have **BRAINS**

85% of all plant life is found in the **OCEAN**

A blue whale is so large that a human could SWIM through its arteries.

The TEA BAG was an accidental invention.

There is no Roman numeral for ZERO

You gain a little bit of height in outer space because there is no GRAVITY

From 0 to 1000, the only number that has the letter ' A ' in it is 'one thousand'.

1000

Earth is **330,330** times smaller than the Sun.

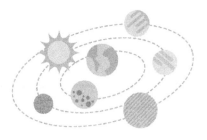

For approximately **2000** years, it was believed that the Sun revolved around the Earth instead of the other way around.

Markings on animal bones indicate that humans have been doing mathematics since around **3000** BC.

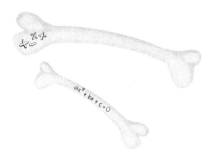

ENGLISH and **MANDARIN** are the world's most popular languages.

Among all shapes with the same perimeter, a CIRCLE has the largest area.

A year isn't exactly 365 days – it's 365. 2564 days! That's why we have a leap year every four years.

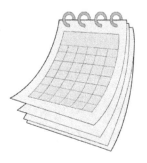

In a room of just 23 people, there's a 50% chance that two people have the same birthday.

There are
43,252,003,274,489,856,000
ways to SCRAMBLE a Rubik's
Cube.

Australia used to be called
NEW HOLLAND

Mount Everest weighs an estimated
357 TRILLION POUNDS

Forests cover **31%** of the world's land surface.

People in Switzerland eat the most **CHOCOLATE**

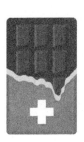

In the United States, **58 MILLION** pounds of chocolate are bought in the week before Valentine's Day.

Usain Bolt, the fastest man in the world, can sprint about 28 miles per hour.

Pi is an irrational number, meaning that it has an **INFINITE** number of digits.

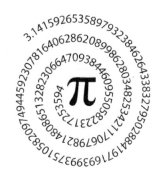

It is impossible to write **Pi** as a fraction.

 There are *292* ways for you to convert a dollar into change.

Brazil was named after a
TREE

 The Great Wall of China is almost
4,000 MILES long.

The word **GOOGOL** was made up by a **9** year old boy.

New York was originally called
NEW AMSTERDAM

Germany shares borders with **9** other countries.

The 2016 **BABY SHARK DANCE** video holds the record for most YouTube views.

There are over **4.1 BiLLiON** active internet users.

The '**SPACE JAM**' movie website is still live.

More than 55% of websites are
in **ENGLISH**

There are 0 rivers in Saudi
Arabia.

Egypt has less pyramids than PERU

4.28 BiLLiON people use their mobile devices to go online.

Mobile traffic to websites is over **51%** of total online traffic.

Over 2.7 billion people use
FACEBOOK

Cyber Monday in 2019 hit record sales of **$9.4 BILLION**

About 98% of Antarctica is covered in ICE

VATICAN CITY is the smallest country in the world.

About 300 million years ago, there were no continents. There was just one mega continent known as
PANGEA

Google was name after googol— a 1 followed by **100** zeroes

Life began in the **OCEAN**

The first computers used to be as big as an entire ROOM

The iPhone has more computing power than the computers that took man to the MOON

The first list of registered domains, created in 1972, looked like IP ADDRESSES

The first network of four computers were linked in **1969**

ARPANET paved the way for the internet in 1969.

Two faraway computers were linked for the first time in **1965**

The company that invented the **MODEM** was a successor of Alexander Graham Bell.

The most common theory for how the universe started is attributed to the BIG BANG Theory.

The human body sheds all its skin every 4 WEEKS

Invented in 1990, ARCHiE was the first version of a search engine.

Your SKiN is the largest body organ!

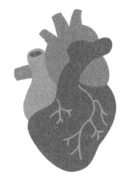

Women's hearts beat faster than MEN'S

Humans spend a third of their lives **ASLEEP**

The human body contains enough fat to make **SEVEN** bars of soap.

Rio de Janeiro translates to River of **JANUARY**

The world's oceans make up **97%** of the water in the world.

Canada contains the most
LAKES in the world

The official national sport of
USA is **BASEBALL**

A day is based on how long it takes for the Earth to do one **full ROTATION**

The universe began approximately **15** billion years ago.

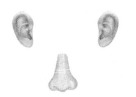

The ears and noses of humans continue to grow throughout the **ENTIRE LIFE**

 Your heart beats about **100,000** times every day!

The human body is made up of about **37 TRILLION** cells.

 Did you know that **99** percent of the DNA is the same in all human beings?

The largest muscle in the human body is the **GLUTEUS MAXIMUS**

Humans are born with about 300 bones, but some fuse together as we grow older. As a result, we only have around **206** left by the time we reach adulthood.

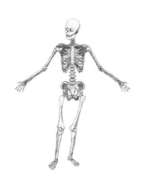

Group **O** blood types can donate blood to anyone while **AB** can receive from anyone.

10 years is called a **DECADE**

Everyone has their own unique

SMELL

100 years is called a CENTURY

 1000 years is called a MILLENNIUM

The longest recorded coma was 37 YEARS long.

 Women were once banned from SMOKING in public.

When you get the hiccups, it will last for an average of **5** minutes.

Columbus didn't actually discover **AMERICA**

Ketchup was sold in the 1830s as **MEDICINE**

Cleopatra was not EGYPTIAN

The fastest hummingbird can flap its wings 80 times per second.

Most people wake up at 7 A.M

If the history of the Earth was compressed into 24 hours, human existence would account for only **40** seconds.

The Black Plague was spread through **FLEAS** that lived on rats.

JOHN ADAMS was the first president to live in the White House.

Calvin Coolidge owned a pair of **LiONS**

The longest period someone has gone without sleep is **11** days.

Before 1970, cola was put in **GLASS** bottles instead of plastic bottles.

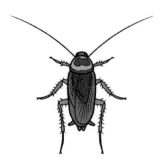

Cockroaches have been around for more than 250 million years.

It is estimated that about 2% of the United States population died during the Civil War, which is a much lower percentage than the number of people killed in other wars.

Dinosaurs roamed the Earth for over 150 MiLLiON years.

SHARKS are some of the oldest animals on Earth.

The **POUND** cake was named that way because it was originally made with a pound of butter, pound of flour, and pound of eggs.

The first face on the $1 bill was not George Washington.

CARS weren't invented in the United States.

Ronald Reagan was a believer in
ASTROLOGY

George Washington never had
WOODEN teeth.

John Adams and Thomas Jefferson died on the
SAME DAY

Thomas Edison is credited with inventing the light **BULB**

BETSY ROSS is credited with designing and sewing the first American flag.

The world's longest French fry is 34 inches long!

Ice cream was once called
"CREAM iCE"

Cucumbers are actually FRUiTS !

Different parts of the world have their own local **CUISINE**

Cutting **ONIONS** releases a gas which causes a stinging sensation when it encounters your eyes.

Pumpkins are usually labelled as vegetables, but they contain seeds and are technically **FRUIT**

Although humans are omnivores (eating both plants and animals), many people choose not to eat meat and fish. They are known as **VEGETARIANS**

Those who don't eat or use any products made from animals (including eggs, dairy products and honey) are known as **VEGANS**

100% VEGAN

Common examples of food **ALLERGIES** include reactions to peanuts, gluten and shellfish.

PESCATARIANS are those people who won't eat any meat, but will still eat fish.

Most supermarket wasabi is **HORSERADISH**

Peanut oil can be used to make **DYNAMITE**

Although bottled water may have an expiration date, it does NOT actually expire.

Strawberries have more vitamin C than oranges.

Pineapples have no relation to PINE

MARGHERITA pizza is named after a queen.

Chickpeas are an excellent source of **PROTEIN**

Bad eggs will **FLOAT**

Ripe cranberries will **BOUNCE**

COFFEE is the main source of antioxidants for Americans.

CASHEWS grow on cashew apples.

The first ice cream cone was invented in **1896**

Lemons float but limes SINK

Chocolate was once used as form of CURRENCY

FOR 8 YEAR OLDS

A typical ear of corn has an ODD number of rows.

Some people have a phobia of color. A PHOBIA means being scared of something.

People are more likely to remember something when it's in

BLACK AND WHITE

Worldwide, **BLUE** is the most common favorite color.

Technically speaking, honey is basically the VOMIT of a bee.

Color affects TASTE

One in every 4 hazelnuts ends up in **NUTELLA**

French fries did not actually originate in France. They originally came from **BELGIUM**

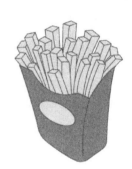

"Bulls hate **RED**" is a total myth.

Neutral colors are also known as **EARTH** tones.

A **DOMINANT** color can change the whole appearance of an image.

Shades and tints are **NOT** the same.

Warm colors are
ENERGIZING

ORANGE JUICE
is one of the main ingredients
in Mountain Dew.

More than 60% of our DNA is
shared with BANANAS

In the eye, there are **NEURONS** that are activated upon seeing red or yellow.

Scarlet is a shade of RED

About 60% of a human is made of WATER

Do you know the difference between. **JAM AND JELLY** ? Jelly is made with fruit juice while, jam is made with fruit.

PHOBIAS are known to be strong, irrational fears that people may feel toward specific triggers.

In simplest terms, the **RAINBOU** consists of red, orange, yellow, green, blue, indigo, and violet (and in that order).

FOR 8 YEAR OLDS

It's obvious how **COLOR** affects our sense of vision, but maybe less apparent that it can also have profound subconscious effects as well.

COLOR PSYCHOLOGY

is the study of how colors affect a person's emotions, thoughts, and even behavior.

BRANDING is a field in which color psychology is often used; businesses use specific colors to influence consumers.

The scientific term for **BRAIN FREEZE** is "sphenopalatine ganglioneuralgia".

FRANCiUM is the rarest element on Earth.

A single strand of Spaghetti is called a **SPAGHETTO**

Argentina is named after the Latin translation of silver: **ARGENTUM**

The most expensive burger in the world is $6000

The famous line in **TiTANiC** from Leonardo DiCaprio, "I'm king of the world!" was improvised.

At birth, a baby panda is smaller than a MOUSE

ICELAND does not have a railway system.

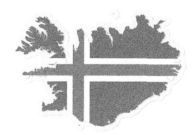

Roman soldiers were often paid i SALT

The average temperature of a fresh **FART** is approximately 99 degrees Fahrenheit or 37 degrees Celsius.

German Chocolate Cake is named after an American baker by the name of Samuel German. It has no affiliation with the country of **GERMANY**

The first toy that was advertised on live television was **MR. POTATO HEAD**

An estimated 50% of all gold ever mined on Earth came from a single plateau in South Africa:
WiTWATERSRAND

The British government coined the slogan, " KEEP CALM and Carry on" during World War 2 in order to motivate citizens to stay strong.

High heels were originally invented for **MEN**

The average human male farts enough in a day to fill up an entire BALLOON

A **GRAPE** will blow up if you put it in the microwave.

There were only 9 developers on the team for GoldenEye 007 for Nintendo 64. Only one of the developers had ever worked on a video game before.

There is an island called **"JUST ENOUGH ROOM"**, where there's just enough room for a tree and a house.

For every human on the planet, there are **200** million bugs.

Sharks can swim up to **45** miles an hour.

 Eggs contain every vitamin except vitamin **C**

It takes **120** raindrops to fill a teaspoon.

 Standing around burns calories. On average, a 150-pound person burns 114 calories per hour while standing and doing **NOTHING**

 **RED** is the first color a baby can see.

We have no idea what color **DiNOSAURS** were

 Pigeons can do **MATH**

A group of porcupines is called a
PRICKLE

A starfish can turn its
stomach INSIDE OUT

Baby flamingos are born
GREY, not pink.

Leave Your Feedback on Amazon

Please think about leaving some feedback via a review on Amazon. It may only take a moment, but it really does mean the world for small businesses like mine.

Even if you did not enjoy this title, please let us know the reason(s) in your review so that we may improve this title and serve you better.

From the Publisher

Hayden Fox's mission is to create premium content for children that will help them expand their vocabulary, grow their imaginations, gain confidence, and share tons of laughs along the way.

Without you, however, this would not be possible, so we sincerely thank you for your purchase and for supporting our company mission.

Printed in Great Britain
by Amazon

21748252R00059